FERRIS CORBETT

When Heaven Hears: A Guide to Intercessory Prayer That Moves Mountains

7 Transformative Principles for Praying Boldly, Breaking Barriers, and Bringing Heaven's Power to Earth

First edition

This book was professionally typeset on Reedsy.
Find out more at reedsy.com

Contents

Preface

Intercessory prayer remains one of the most profound and transformative ways to impact lives and circumstances in a world filled with division, uncertainty, and unrelenting challenges. Yet, many believers are unaware of the immense power they wield when they step into the sacred role of intercessor. Intercessors have been the quiet warriors of faith, standing in the gap for individuals, communities, and nations for centuries. Their prayers have sparked revivals, healed broken lives, and delivered miraculous breakthroughs.

When Heaven Hears: A Guide to Intercessory Prayer That Moves Mountains is born out of a deep conviction that intercessory prayer is not just for the spiritually elite—it is a calling for every believer. Whether you are a seasoned prayer warrior or someone just discovering the beauty of intercession, this book is designed to equip and inspire you to embrace this life-changing ministry. Through Scripture, practical guidance, and real-life testimonies, this book will take you on a journey to discover how your prayers can become a powerful force for good, not only in your life but also in the lives of those you intercede for.

Why this book? Over the years, I have encountered countless individuals who yearn to pray effectively but feel hindered by doubts, distractions, or a lack of understanding. Many believe their prayers lack power or are unworthy to approach God boldly. These misconceptions have kept countless believers from fulfilling their divine purpose as intercessors. I hope that *When Heaven Hears* will shatter these barriers and ignite a fresh passion for prayer.

This book is structured around seven transformative principles that will guide you to pray boldly, align with God's will, and experience the supernatural power of intercessory prayer. Each principle is rooted in Scripture, brought to life through real-world applications, and designed to deepen your faith. As you read, you will discover how to stand in the gap for others, persist in prayer despite challenges, and access the promises of God with unwavering confidence.

Ultimately, my prayer for you as a reader is simple: this book will inspire you to become a catalyst for change, an agent of hope, and a vessel of God's love through prayer. May the pages ahead encourage and empower you to intercede boldly, bringing heaven's power to earth.

Introduction

Why Intercessory Prayer Matters

When was the last time you prayed for someone else? Not a fleeting thought or a casual mention but a heartfelt, focused prayer where you stood in faith, believing for a breakthrough on their behalf? Intercessory prayer is one of the most selfless acts a believer can engage in. It shifts the focus away from our personal needs and aligns our hearts with God's purpose for others. It allows us to partner with God in ways that transform lives and circumstances beyond what we can imagine.

The Privilege of Partnership

Intercessory prayer is not a burden but a privilege. It is an invitation to partner with the Creator of the universe in shaping destinies, restoring hope, and advancing His kingdom. Think about that for a moment: your prayers have the power to move mountains, heal broken hearts, and change the trajectory of nations. This is not just poetic rhetoric but a divine reality backed by Scripture.

Consider the story of Moses interceding for the Israelites after they had sinned by worshiping the golden calf. God, in His righteous anger, was ready to bring judgment upon them, but Moses stood in the gap, pleading for mercy. His prayers changed the outcome (Exodus 32:11-14). Similarly, in the New Testament, we see Paul constantly interceding for the churches, asking God to strengthen their faith, grant them wisdom, and protect them from harm (Ephesians 1:15-19, Philippians 1:9-11).

These examples are not meant to intimidate but to inspire. The same God who responded to Moses and Paul listens to your prayers today. He invites you to stand in the gap for your family, community, and the world. This is the heart of intercession: stepping into the gap between God's promises and the needs of others.

Breaking Barriers Through Prayer

For many, the idea of intercessory prayer feels daunting. Perhaps you feel unworthy, unsure, or unequipped to pray for others. Maybe you have been discouraged by previously unanswered prayers in the past or feel uncertain about how to pray effectively. Let me reassure you: intercessory prayer is not about having the perfect words or being a spiritual giant. It is about having a heart willing to trust God and persist in faith.

Through each chapter and section of this book, we will explore the barriers that often hinder intercessors and how to overcome them. Whether it is the fear of failure, distractions that steal your focus, or doubts that creep in when answers do not come immediately, you will learn how to navigate these challenges and persevere in prayer. You will also discover that intercessory prayer is not a solo endeavor. The Holy Spirit is your constant companion, guiding your prayers and interceding on your behalf when words fail (Romans 8:26-27).

The Seven Principles of Transformative Prayer

At the core of this book are seven principles that will transform your understanding and practice of intercessory prayer:

1. **Faith That Moves Mountains**: Learn how to pray boldly through faith, trusting God for the impossible.
2. **Aligning With God's Will**: Discover how to discern God's will and pray in agreement with His purposes.
3. **Praying With Boldness**: Overcome fear and hesitation and confidentially approach God's throne.
4. **Persistence in Prayer**: Cultivate the discipline of praying persistently despite delays or setbacks.
5. **Standing in the Gap for Others**: Embrace the privilege of interceding for individuals, communities, and nations.
6. **Using Scripture in Prayer**: Harness the power of God's Word to guide

and amplify your prayers.

7. **Spiritual Warfare in Intercession**: Equip yourself for the spiritual battles that accompany effective intercession.

Each principle builds upon the last, creating a framework that will empower you to intercede with purpose and passion. By the end of this journey, you will understand the mechanics of intercession but also experience its transformative power in your own life.

A Word of Encouragement

As you embark on this journey, I want to remind you that intercessory prayer is a growing process. You do not have to master everything overnight. Like any spiritual discipline, it requires practice, patience, and persistence. But rest assured, the rewards are worth it. When you see the lives of those, you pray for being changed. When you witness breakthroughs that can only be attributed to God's intervention, and when your faith deepens. As a result, you will understand why intercessory prayer matters so profoundly.

The purpose of this book is not merely a how-to guide but an invitation to step into a deeper relationship with God. While interceding for others, you will find yourself drawn closer to His heart. You will see His faithfulness in action and develop a deeper understanding of His love for humanity.

Are you ready to take your prayers to the next level? Are you willing to stand in the gap and see what God can do through your faith? If so, let us begin this journey together. Heaven is waiting, and mountains are ready to move. Let us step boldly into the intercessory prayer ministry by answering the call!

1

Chapter 1

Chapter 1: Building a Foundation for Effective Intercession

Intercessory prayer is a profound and transformative ministry. However, one must first lay a solid foundation. This foundation will allow one to wield the power of intercessory effectively. Just as a builder prepares the ground before constructing a house, we must also prepare our hearts, minds, and spirits for the work of intercession. This chapter explores the foundational principles that every intercessor needs to embrace: understanding their role, engaging in spiritual preparation, and establishing a consistent prayer life.

Section 1: Understanding the Role of an Intercessor

The Biblical Mandate for Intercession

Intercession is not merely a personal calling. It is a divine mandate given to every believer. Throughout Scripture, God calls His people to stand in the gap for others, to advocate on their behalf, and to seek His intervention in their lives. One of the most powerful examples is found in Ezekiel 22:30, where God laments, *"I looked for someone among them who would build up the wall and stand before me in the gap on behalf of the land so I would not have to destroy it, but I found no one."* This verse underscores the critical role of the intercessor

4

in bridging the gap between God's holiness and humanity's need for mercy.

Other examples abound. Abraham interceded for Sodom and Gomorrah, pleading for God's mercy even when the cities were steeped in sin (Genesis 18:16-33). Moses, too, stood in the gap for the Israelites, interceding when God's anger burned against them for their idolatry (Exodus 32:11-14). These stories highlight the courage and faith required of an intercessor and the profound impact of their prayers.

As intercessors, we are called to follow these biblical examples, recognizing that our prayers are not just words spoken into the void. They are acts of obedience, partnership, and love, rooted in the knowledge that God listens and responds to those who seek Him on behalf of others.

The Heart of Compassion in Prayer

Intercessory prayer flows from a heart of compassion. It is impossible to pray effectively for others without feeling their burdens, empathizing with their struggles, and longing for their deliverance. Jesus Himself demonstrated this compassion repeatedly. In John 17, often known as the High Priestly Prayer, Jesus interceded for His disciples and all believers, asking the Father to protect, sanctify, and unify them. His prayer was born out of deep love and concern for His followers.

As intercessors, we are called to mirror this heart of compassion. This means approaching prayer not as an obligation but as an act of love. It requires us to step outside our concerns and immerse ourselves in the needs of others, trusting that God's power will work through our petitions to bring about His purposes.

Intercession as a Lifelong Calling

Intercession is not a seasonal activity or a temporary phase in one's spiritual journey; it is a lifelong calling. It requires commitment, perseverance, and a willingness to grow continually in faith and understanding. The Apostle Paul exemplified this dedication, consistently praying for the churches he had established. In Colossians 1:9, he writes, *"We have not stopped praying for you."* His steadfast commitment to intercessory prayer demonstrates that this ministry is not a one-time event but an ongoing responsibility.

Embracing intercession as a lifelong calling also means being open to God's leading. There will be seasons when the burdens of intercession feel heavy and times when the answers to our prayers seem delayed. Yet, in these moments of perseverance, we grow closer to God, deepen our trust in Him, and witness His faithfulness.

Section 2: Spiritual Preparation

Cleansing the Heart and Spirit Before Prayer

We must prepare our hearts and spirits before entering into intercessory prayer. Psalm 24:3-4 reminds us, *"Who may ascend the mountain of the Lord? Who may stand in his holy place? The one who has clean hands and a pure heart."* Effective intercession requires us to approach God humbly, seeking forgiveness for our sins and aligning ourselves with His will.

Confession and repentance are vital aspects of this cleansing process. When we acknowledge our shortcomings and ask God for mercy, we position ourselves to intercede with purity and sincerity. Also, inviting the Holy Spirit to search our hearts and reveal any hidden areas of sin or bitterness ensures that nothing hinders our prayers.

Cultivating a Lifestyle of Holiness

Holiness is not a requirement exclusive to intercessors, but it is especially crucial for those who stand in the gap for others. A lifestyle of holiness involves daily surrender to God, obedience to His Word, and a commitment to living in alignment with His character. This does not mean perfection but striving to reflect Christ in our thoughts, actions, and relationships.

Holiness also includes being mindful of what we allow into our hearts and minds. Intercessors must guard against distractions, negative influences, and anything that weakens their spiritual resolve. By staying rooted in Scripture and maintaining an active relationship with God, we cultivate the needed spiritual strength to persevere in prayer.

Overcoming Fear and Doubt in Intercession

Fear and doubt are two of the greatest obstacles to effective intercessory prayer. Many intercessors struggle with questions such as, "What if my prayers don't make a difference?" or "Am I qualified to intercede for others?" These doubts can paralyze and prevent us from stepping into our God-given role.

To overcome fear and doubt, we must remember that the power of intercessory prayer does not come from us—it comes from God. Our role is not to perform miracles but to seek His will and trust in His ability to bring about change. Meditating on verses such as 2 Timothy 1:7, which states, *"For God has not given us a spirit of fear, but of power and of love and of a sound mind,"* helps to build our confidence and remind us that God equips us for the task at hand.

Section 3: Developing a Consistent Prayer Life

Establishing a Daily Routine of Prayer

Consistency is key to effective intercession. Just as athletes train regularly to build endurance, intercessors must cultivate a disciplined prayer life to stay spiritually sharp. To ensure that we remain connected to God and prepared to intercede when needed, we must make it a routine to pray daily.

A practical way to develop this routine is to set aside specific times each day for prayer. Whether in the morning, during lunch, or before bed, having a designated time helps to create a pattern of praying that becomes second nature. Additionally, creating a quiet, distraction-free space for prayer allows us to focus fully on God and the needs we are petitioning Him for.

Using Scripture as a Foundation for Prayer

Scripture is a powerful tool in intercessory prayer. It provides guidance and encouragement and serves as a foundation for our petitions. By praying God's Word, we align our requests with His promises and declare His truth over the situations we are interceding for.

For example, when praying for someone's healing, we can draw on verses like Isaiah 53:5, which says, *"By His wounds we are healed."* When interceding for peace in a family or community, we can claim Philippians 4:7: *"And the peace of God, which transcends all understanding, will guard your hearts and your minds in Christ Jesus."* When we use Scripture in this way, it strengthens our faith and ensures that our prayers are rooted in God's will.

Journaling and Tracking Prayer Requests

Journaling is an invaluable practice for intercessors. By recording prayer requests, we can keep track of the needs we are lifting before God and remain intentional about our intercession. Journaling also allows us to document answers to prayer, which provides a source of encouragement and a reminder of God's faithfulness.

A simple way to start is by keeping a notebook or digital log where you write down specific prayer requests, the date you began praying for them, and any updates or answers that come over time. Reviewing these entries periodically can provide a sense of gratitude and motivate you to continue interceding with faith and perseverance.

By understanding your role as an intercessor, engaging in spiritual preparation, and cultivating a consistent prayer life, you can build a strong foundation for effective intercessory prayer. These principles will deepen your relationship with God and empower you to stand in the gap with boldness and confidence, trusting that your prayers will move mountains.

2

Chapter 2

Chapter 2: The First Principle—Faith That Moves Mountains

Faith is the cornerstone of intercessory prayer. It is the channel through which we access God's power and the foundation upon which all effective prayers are built. Without faith, prayer becomes little more than wishful thinking, but with faith, even the most insurmountable challenges can be overcome. This chapter explores how faith fuels intercessory prayer, how to pray with expectancy, and how to strengthen your faith to see God move in miraculous ways.

Section 1: What Is Faith-Fueled Prayer?

Faith as the Foundation of Intercession

Faith-fueled prayer begins with an unshakable belief in God's ability and willingness to answer prayer. Hebrews 11:1 defines faith as *"confidence in what we hope for and assurance about what we do not see."* This confidence forms the basis of intercessory prayer, allowing us to approach God boldly and trust Him to work even when circumstances seem impossible.

The Bible is filled with stories of intercessors whose faith changed the course of history. One example is Elijah, who prayed fervently for rain after a long drought (1 Kings 18:41–46). Elijah's faith in God's promise to send rain drove him to pray persistently, and his prayers were answered. Similarly, Jesus emphasized the power of faith in intercession, teaching His disciples in Mark 11:23, *"Truly I tell you, if anyone says to this mountain, 'Go, throw yourself into the sea,' and does not doubt in their heart but believes that what they say will happen, it will be done for them."*

As intercessors, we must approach prayer with bold, mountain-moving faith. It is not about the strength of our own will but about trusting in God's infinite power and faithfulness.

The Role of Belief in Unlocking Miracles

Belief is the catalyst that transforms ordinary prayers into extraordinary outcomes. When we believe in God's promises and trust His character, our prayers align with His will and activate His power. Jesus repeatedly highlighted the connection between belief and miracles, as seen in Matthew 9:29 when He told two blind men, *"According to your faith, let it be done to you."* Their healing did not come from them depending on their effort but from their belief in Jesus' ability to heal.

Intercessors who believe in God's power often witness miraculous breakthroughs—not because of their righteousness but because they trust Him. Doors are open for God to work in ways that surpass human understanding when we have this kind of faith. When we pray with belief, we give God room to perform the miraculous.

Why Doubt Weakens Intercession

Doubt is the enemy of faith and one of the greatest obstacles to effective intercession. James 1:6–7 warns, *"But when you ask, you must believe and not doubt, because the one who doubts is like a wave of the sea, blown and tossed by the wind. That person should not expect to receive anything from the Lord."* Doubt diminishes our confidence in God and undermines the effectiveness of our prayers.

While doubt is a natural human response, we must resist letting it take root in our hearts. The antidote to doubt is meditating on God's faithfulness, reminding ourselves of His past works, and standing firmly on His promises. By replacing doubt with trust, we strengthen our faith and position ourselves to see God's power at work.

Section 2: Praying With Expectancy

Visualizing the Answer Before You See It

Faith-fueled prayer involves visualizing the answer even before it becomes a reality. This is not a form of wishful thinking but an expression of trust in God's ability to fulfill His promises. Hebrews 11:6 reminds us that *"without faith, it is impossible to please God because anyone who comes to him must believe that he exists and that he rewards those who earnestly seek him."*

When we visualize God's answer, we align our hearts with His will and cultivate expectancy. This practice strengthens our belief and helps us pray with greater conviction. For example, if you are interceding for someone's healing, envision them restored and whole. If praying for financial provision, imagine God meeting their needs abundantly.

Trusting God's Timing and Wisdom

While expectancy is vital, it must be accompanied by trust in God's timing and wisdom. Sometimes, the answers to our prayers do not come as quickly or in the way we expect. Isaiah 55:8-9 reminds us, *"'For my thoughts are not your thoughts, neither are your ways my ways,' declares the Lord. 'As the heavens are higher than the earth, so are my ways higher than your ways and my thoughts than your thoughts.'"*

Trusting God's timing means surrendering our expectations and acknowlededging His plans are always best. It involves patience, perseverance, and a willingness to wait for His perfect will to unfold. During the waiting period, our faith is refined, and our relationship with God deepens.

Turning Small Prayers Into Bold Requests

Faith-filled intercession requires us to move beyond small, timid prayers and step into bold, audacious requests. God delights in big prayers because they reflect our belief in His greatness. In Ephesians 3:20, Paul writes, *"Now to him who is able to do immeasurably more than all we ask or imagine, according to his power that is at work within us."* This verse encourages us to pray boldly, knowing that God's power far exceeds our comprehension.

For example, instead of praying, "God, if it is Your will, please provide for this need," pray with confidence: "God, I trust You to supply all their needs according to Your riches in glory." Bold prayers demonstrate faith and invite God to move mightily.

Section 3: Strengthening Your Faith in Prayer

Studying the Promises of God

One of the most effective ways to strengthen faith in prayer is by studying and meditating on God's promises. The Bible is filled with assurances of God's faithfulness, power, and love, all of which serve as a foundation for our prayers. For example:

- *"And my God will meet all your needs according to the riches of his glory in Christ Jesus"* (Philippians 4:19).
- *"The prayer of a righteous person is powerful and effective"* (James 5:16).
- *"If you believe, you will receive whatever you ask for in prayer"* (Matthew 21:22).

By immersing ourselves in these promises, we reinforce our confidence in God's ability to answer prayer and align our requests with His Word.

Overcoming Setbacks and Unanswered Prayers

Setbacks and unanswered prayers can test our faith and discourage us from continuing in intercession. However, these challenges are an opportunity to grow stronger in faith. When prayers seem unanswered, it is crucial to remember that God's silence is not His absence. He may be working behind the scenes in ways we cannot yet see.

Romans 8:28 assures us that *"in all things, God works for the good of those who love him, who have been called according to his purpose."* This promise reminds us that even when outcomes are not as we expected, God's plans are always for our ultimate good. By holding onto this truth, we can overcome discouragement and persist in prayer.

Celebrating Small Wins to Build Faith

Celebrating small wins is a practical way to build faith and maintain motivation in intercession. When we acknowledge even the smallest answers to prayer, we cultivate gratitude and reinforce our belief in God's faithfulness. For example, if you are praying for someone's healing and they experience a minor improvement, rejoice and thank God for that progress.

Documenting these small victories in a prayer journal can also serve as a source of encouragement during times of doubt or waiting. By reflecting on God's past faithfulness, we strengthen our resolve to trust Him for even greater breakthroughs.

Faith-fueled prayer is at the heart of effective intercession. By understanding the role of belief, praying with expectancy, and actively strengthening our faith, we position ourselves to see God move in powerful ways. Faith is not just a feeling; it is an active, unwavering trust in the One who can do far more than we can ask or imagine. Let this principle guide your prayers as you step into the role of an intercessor and witness the mountains move before you.

3

Chapter 3

Chapter 3: The Second Principle—Aligning With God's Will

Effective intercession is not about bending God's will to fit our desires but about aligning our prayers with His perfect plan. Aligning with God's will is foundational for intercessory prayer because it ensures that our petitions are rooted in His eternal purposes. This chapter explores how to understand God's will through Scripture, listen for His voice, and surrender our desires to pray in harmony with His divine plan.

Section 1: The Importance of Divine Alignment

Understanding God's Will Through Scripture

Scripture is the ultimate guide for understanding God's will. It reveals His character, His promises, and His purposes for humanity. When our prayers are grounded in the Word of God, we can be confident that they align with His will. As 1 John 5:14 assures us, *"This is the confidence we have in approaching God: that if we ask anything according to his will, he hears us."*

To discern God's will through Scripture:

1. **Study the overarching themes of God's plan.** God's will often centers

14

on love, redemption, justice, and mercy. When we pray for these things, we are aligning with His heart.

2. **Seek specific promises and guidance.** For example, if praying for provision, turn to Philippians 4:19: *"And my God will meet all your needs according to the riches of his glory in Christ Jesus."*

3. **Allow Scripture to refine your motives.** Hebrews 4:12 reminds us that *"the word of God is alive and active. Sharper than any double-edged sword, it penetrates even to dividing soul and spirit, joints and marrow; it judges the thoughts and attitudes of the heart."* The Bible not only guides our prayers but also purifies them.

Praying in Agreement With God's Purposes

Praying in agreement with God's purposes involves seeking His glory above all else. The Lord's Prayer provides a model for this mindset: *"Your kingdom come, your will be done, on earth as it is in heaven"* (Matthew 6:10). This prayer reflects a heart that desires God's will to prevail over personal preferences.

When we pray in alignment with God's purposes, our intercession becomes a powerful partnership with Him. Consider the examples of biblical intercessors like Daniel, who prayed fervently for the fulfillment of God's promise to restore Israel (Daniel 9:1-19). His prayer was rooted in God's covenant and promises, demonstrating how aligning with God's purposes can lead to extraordinary outcomes.

Recognizing the Signs of Misaligned Prayers

Not all prayers are aligned with God's will, and recognizing when our prayers are misaligned is essential for effective intercession. Signs of misaligned prayers include:

1. **Self-centered motives.** James 4:3 warns, *"When you ask, you do not receive, because you ask with wrong motives, that you may spend what you get on your pleasures."*

2. **A lack of peace.** When our prayers are outside God's will, we often feel restless or uncertain. The peace of God serves as an indicator of alignment

(Philippians 4:7).

3. **Persistent obstacles.** While challenges are part of life, repeated road-blocks may signal that our prayers need reevaluation.

Realigning our prayers with God's will requires humility, a willingness to listen, and a commitment to seeking His guidance.

Section 2: Listening for God's Voice

How to Hear God Speak During Prayer

Listening for God's voice is a vital aspect of intercessory prayer. While God speaks in various ways—through Scripture, circumstances, and others—prayer provides a unique opportunity to hear Him directly. Jesus affirmed this in John 10:27: *"My sheep listen to my voice; I know them, and they follow me."*

To hear God speak during prayer:

1. **Create a quiet, distraction-free environment.** Silence allows you to focus on His presence and voice.
2. **Pray for discernment.** Ask the Holy Spirit to open your heart and mind to God's message.
3. **Pay attention to impressions or thoughts.** God often communicates through subtle nudges that align with His Word.

Hearing God's voice takes practice and patience, but the more we listen, the clearer His guidance becomes.

Discerning God's Will Through the Holy Spirit

The Holy Spirit plays a critical role in helping intercessors discern God's will. Romans 8:26-27 explains, *"The Spirit helps us in our weakness. We do not know what we ought to pray for, but the Spirit himself intercedes for us through wordless groans."* The Spirit aligns our prayers with God's will, even when we lack clarity.

Practical steps for discerning God's will through the Spirit include:

1. **Inviting the Spirit's guidance before prayer.** Begin by surrendering your agenda and asking for His leading.
2. **Being sensitive to promptings.** The Spirit may guide you to pray for specific people, situations, or outcomes.
3. **Trusting His intercession.** Even when words fail, the Spirit intercedes on your behalf, ensuring your prayers align with God's purposes.

The Role of Silence and Waiting in Intercession

Silence and waiting are integral to aligning with God's will. In our fast-paced world, we often rush through prayer, missing the opportunity to hear from God. Psalm 46:10 reminds us, *"Be still, and know that I am God."*

Waiting on God during prayer involves:

1. **Resisting the urge to fill the silence.** Allow God to speak without interrupting by entertaining your thoughts.
2. **Meditating on His Word.** Reflecting on Scripture during moments of stillness helps attune your spirit to His voice.
3. **Practicing patience.** Answers may not come immediately, but waiting demonstrates trust in God's timing.

Section 3: Surrendering Personal Desires

Letting Go of Selfish Ambitions

Intercessory prayer requires surrendering selfish ambitions and aligning our desires with God's. Philippians 2:3-4 encourages us to *"do nothing out of selfish ambition or vain conceit. Rather, in humility, value others above yourselves, not looking to your interests but each of you to the interests of the others."*

Letting go of selfish ambitions means:

1. **Prioritizing God's glory over personal gain.** Ask, "Does this prayer serve God's kingdom or my own?"
2. **Praying with humility.** Acknowledge that God's wisdom far surpasses your understanding.

3. **Releasing control.** Trust that God's plans are better than your own, even when they differ from your expectations.

Praying "Thy Will Be Done" With Trust

One of the most powerful prayers an intercessor can offer is, *"Thy will be done."* This prayer reflects complete trust in God's sovereignty and goodness. Jesus modeled this in the Garden of Gethsemane when He prayed, *"Father, if you are willing, take this cup from me; yet not my will, but yours be done"* (Luke 22:42).

Praying "Thy will be done" requires:

1. **Releasing the outcome to God.** Surrender your desired result and trust Him to provide what is best.
2. **Believing in His character.** Trust that God's plans are always for your ultimate good (Romans 8:28).
3. **Cultivating peace.** Let go of anxiety and rest in the assurance that God is in control.

Finding Joy in God's Sovereign Plan

When we align our prayers with God's will, we find joy in His sovereignty. Even when His plans differ from ours, we can trust that they are perfect. Psalm 37:4 encourages us to *"take delight in the Lord, and he will give you the desires of your heart."* This verse reminds us that when we delight in God, our desires begin to align with His.

Finding joy in God's plan involves:

1. **Celebrating His faithfulness.** Reflect on how He has worked in your life and the lives of others.
2. **Reframing challenges as opportunities for growth.** Trust that even difficulties are part of His divine purpose.
3. **Rejoicing in His presence.** True joy comes from knowing and trusting God, regardless of circumstances.

Aligning with God's will is the key to powerful intercession. By understanding His will through Scripture, listening for His voice, and surrendering our desires, we position ourselves to pray in harmony with His purposes. This alignment transforms our prayers from wishful requests into powerful declarations that bring heaven's power to earth. As you embrace this principle, you will discover the peace, joy, and effectiveness that come from praying according to God's perfect will.

4

Chapter 4

Chapter 4: The Third Principle—Praying With Boldness

Boldness in prayer is a hallmark of effective intercession. It reflects unwavering confidence in God's power, love, and willingness to act. Bold prayer is not about arrogance but about trusting in the authority God has given His children. This chapter explores biblical examples of bold prayer, addresses how to overcome fear and hesitation, and teaches how to pray with authority and confidence.

Section 1: Boldness in Biblical Examples

Elijah's Confidence in Calling Fire From Heaven

Elijah's prayer on Mount Carmel is one of the most dramatic examples of bold intercession in the Bible. Facing 450 prophets of Baal, Elijah called upon the Lord to send fire from heaven to prove His supremacy and turn Israel's hearts back to Him (1 Kings 18:36-39). Elijah prayed with confidence because he knew he was aligned with God's will and purpose.

Elijah's boldness teaches us several key lessons:

1. **Know God's character.** Elijah trusted in God's power and faithfulness,

which gave him the confidence to pray boldly.

2. **Step out in faith.** Bold prayers require us to take risks, trusting that God will respond.
3. **Pray for God's glory.** Elijah's prayer was not for personal gain but for God's name to be glorified.

The Persistent Widow: A Lesson in Perseverance

Jesus highlighted the importance of bold and persistent prayer through the parable of the persistent widow (Luke 18:1-8). The widow repeatedly petitioned an unjust judge for justice, and her persistence ultimately won her case. Jesus used this parable to encourage His followers to pray boldly and persistently, assuring them that if an unjust judge would respond, how much more would God answer His children's prayers?

Key takeaways from the widow's example include:

1. **Don't give up.** Bold prayer is not deterred by delays or obstacles.
2. **Be persistent.** Repeated petitions show faith in God's willingness to act.
3. **Trust God's justice.** The widow trusted that her plea for justice would be answered, and so should we.

Paul's Courage in Praying for Miracles

The Apostle Paul demonstrated boldness in prayer throughout his ministry. In Acts 28:8, Paul prayed for the healing of Publius's father, and the man was cured of fever and dysentery. Paul's prayers were fearless because they were grounded in his faith in God's power and his desire to advance the gospel.

Paul's example shows us:

1. **Pray with purpose.** Paul's bold prayers were often linked to his mission of spreading the gospel.
2. **Trust God's ability to work through you.** Paul believed that God could use him as an instrument of His power.
3. **Be fearless in public prayer.** Paul prayed boldly in the presence of others, showing faith in God's ability to act.

Section 2: Overcoming Fear and Hesitation

Replacing Fear With Faith in God's Power

Fear often holds believers back from praying boldly. This fear may stem from doubts about God's willingness to answer, concerns about appearing presumptuous, or insecurities about their worthiness. To replace fear with faith, we must focus on God's character and promises.

Steps to overcome fear:

1. **Meditate on God's faithfulness.** Reflect on verses like 2 Timothy 1:7: *"For God has not given us a spirit of fear, but of power and of love and of a sound mind."*
2. **Remember past answers to prayer.** Reflecting on God's faithfulness in the past builds confidence for future prayers.
3. **Declare God's promises.** Speaking Scripture over your fears helps reinforce your trust in God.

How to Approach God's Throne With Confidence

Hebrews 4:16 encourages believers to *"approach God's throne of grace with confidence, so that we may receive mercy and find grace to help us in our time of need."* Bold prayer begins with the understanding that we have the right to approach God as His children, not as strangers.

How to cultivate confidence in prayer:

1. **Understand your identity in Christ.** As children of God, we are heirs to His promises (Romans 8:17).
2. **Focus on God's grace.** Boldness is not about our worthiness but about God's unmerited favor.
3. **Pray with expectation.** Trust that God delights in hearing and answering your prayers.

Breaking the Chains of Intimidation

Intimidation is another barrier to bold prayer. It may come from spiritual opposition, feelings of inadequacy, or fear of failure. Breaking free from intimidation involves relying on God's power rather than your strength.

Practical steps to overcome intimidation:

1. **Rely on the Holy Spirit.** The Spirit empowers believers to pray with boldness (Acts 4:31).
2. **Focus on God, not the problem.** Shifting your perspective from the size of the problem to the greatness of God reduces fear.
3. **Speak truth over intimidation.** Declare Scriptures like Philippians 4:13: *"I can do all this through him who gives me strength."*

Section 3: Speaking With Authority

Declaring God's Promises Over Circumstances

Bold prayer involves declaring God's promises over the situations we are interceding for. This is not about forcing God's hand but about standing on His Word and aligning our prayers with His will. For example, when praying for healing, you might declare Isaiah 53:5: *"By His wounds we are healed."*

How to declare God's promises:

1. **Identify relevant Scriptures.** Find verses that apply to the situation you're praying about.
2. **Speak the Word aloud.** Verbalizing Scripture reinforces your faith and aligns your prayer with God's truth.
3. **Pray with conviction.** Trust that God's Word will not return void (Isaiah 55:11).

Using the Name of Jesus in Spiritual Warfare

The name of Jesus carries unparalleled authority in spiritual warfare. In John 14:13-14, Jesus assures His followers, *"And I will do whatever you ask in my name, so that the Father may be glorified in the Son."* Praying in Jesus' name is not a formula but a declaration of His authority and power.

How to use the name of Jesus effectively:

1. **Understand its significance.** The name of Jesus represents His authority and victory over the grave, sin, death, and the enemy.
2. **Use it in faith.** When you invoke Jesus' name, believe in its power to overcome every obstacle.
3. **Apply it to specific situations.** Declare Jesus' name over areas of bondage, sickness, or spiritual attack.

Understanding Your Authority as a Believer

As believers, we have been given authority through Christ to intercede boldly and combat spiritual forces. Ephesians 2:6 reminds us that we are seated with Christ in heavenly places, sharing in His authority.

Key aspects of your authority as a believer:

1. **Rooted in Christ.** Your authority comes from your position in Christ, not your merit.
2. **Exercised through prayer.** Bold prayers activate the authority God has entrusted to you.
3. **Confirmed by Scripture.** Verses like Luke 10:19 affirm your authority: *"I have given you authority to trample on snakes and scorpions and to overcome all the power of the enemy."*

Praying with boldness is an essential principle of intercessory prayer. By learning from biblical examples, overcoming fear, and speaking with authority, you can approach God's throne with confidence and trust in His power to act. Bold prayers not only reflect faith in God but also invite Him to move in extraordinary ways, bringing heaven's power to earth. Let this principle empower you to intercede fearlessly and see the miraculous unfold.

5

Chapter 5

Chapter 5: The Fourth Principle—Persistence in Prayer

Persistence is a hallmark of effective intercession. It is the discipline of continuing in prayer, even when answers seem delayed, circumstances grow challenging, or discouragement looms. Persistent prayer is not about wearing God down but about aligning ourselves with His timing and purposes while demonstrating unwavering faith. This chapter delves into the importance of persistence, how to cultivate a resilient mindset, and practical tips for staying the course in long-term intercession.

Section 1: Why Persistence Matters

Breaking Through Spiritual Resistance

Persistent prayer often involves spiritual warfare. In the unseen realm, there are forces of opposition that can hinder or delay answers to prayer. Daniel 10 provides a vivid example of this dynamic. When Daniel prayed for understanding, his answer was delayed by 21 days due to spiritual resistance. An angel eventually delivered the message, explaining that the prince of Persia had opposed him (Daniel 10:12-13).

This story highlights the importance of persistence:

1. **Prayer is a spiritual weapon.** Persistent prayer helps to break through barriers that might otherwise hinder God's work.
2. **Perseverance demonstrates faith.** Continuing in prayer shows that we trust God's ultimate victory over any opposition.
3. **God's timing is perfect.** Persistence does not rush God but aligns us with His perfect plan.

Understanding Delays in God's Answers

God's delays are not denials. Sometimes, the answers to our prayers take time because God is working in ways we cannot yet see. This could involve preparing our hearts, aligning circumstances, or accomplishing purposes beyond our understanding. Habakkuk 2:3 reminds us, *"For the revelation awaits an appointed time; it speaks of the end and will not prove false. Though it lingers, wait for it; it will certainly come and will not delay."*

Reasons for delays:

1. **Spiritual preparation.** God may be preparing you or others involved to receive the answer.
2. **Character development.** Delays often build patience, faith, and trust in God's sovereignty.
3. **God's greater purpose.** Sometimes, the answer is tied to a larger plan that requires perfect timing.

The Power of "Keep Knocking" Prayer

In Luke 11:5–10, Jesus tells the parable of a persistent friend who knocks on a neighbor's door at midnight, asking for bread. Despite the inconvenience, the neighbor eventually gets up and provides what is needed. Jesus concludes, *"Ask and it will be given to you; seek and you will find; knock and the door will be opened to you."*

This parable teaches us that persistent prayer:

1. **Reflects bold faith.** Persistence shows that we believe God will answer.
2. **Engages God's promises.** The act of "knocking" demonstrates trust in

God's willingness to respond.

3. **Builds a deeper relationship.** Persistent prayer draws us closer to God as we continually seek Him.

Section 2: Developing a Persistent Mindset

Staying Committed Despite Discouragement

Discouragement is one of the greatest challenges to persistence in prayer. Unanswered prayers, delays, or apparent setbacks can lead to frustration or even doubt. However, staying committed requires focusing on God's faithfulness rather than the current circumstances.

Strategies for staying committed:

1. **Remember God's past faithfulness.** Reflect on previous answers to prayer as evidence of His reliability.
2. **Focus on His promises.** Anchor your prayers in Scriptures that affirm His faithfulness and timing.
3. **Seek encouragement.** Share your burdens with fellow believers who can pray with and for you.

Turning Setbacks Into Renewed Determination

Setbacks in prayer are inevitable, but they do not have to derail your faith. Instead, they can serve as opportunities for growth and renewed commitment. James 1:2-4 encourages us to consider trials as opportunities for perseverance, which leads to maturity.

Turning setbacks into determination:

1. **Reframe challenges.** View setbacks as moments where God is working in ways you cannot yet see.
2. **Pray with transparency.** Be honest with God about your frustrations, and invite Him to strengthen your faith.
3. **Declare God's sovereignty.** Affirm that He is in control and trust that His purposes will prevail.

Building Endurance Through Scripture

The Bible is a powerful resource for developing endurance in prayer. Stories of persistent intercessors and promises of God's faithfulness provide encouragement to persevere.

Key Scriptures for endurance:

1. Romans 12:12: *"Be joyful in hope, patient in affliction, faithful in prayer."*
2. Galatians 6:9: *"Let us not become weary in doing good, for at the proper time we will reap a harvest if we do not give up."*
3. Matthew 7:7: *"Ask and it will be given to you; seek and you will find; knock and the door will be opened to you."*

Meditating on these verses and incorporating them into your prayers can sustain you during times of waiting.

Section 3: Practical Tips for Persistent Prayer

Setting Prayer Goals and Staying Accountable

Setting clear goals for your prayer life can help you stay focused and consistent. Goals provide direction, while accountability ensures that you remain committed to the discipline of intercession.

Practical steps for setting prayer goals:

1. **Identify specific areas of focus.** List the people, situations, or needs you feel called to intercede for.
2. **Establish a routine.** Dedicate specific times each day or week for focused prayer.
3. **Find an accountability partner.** Share your goals with someone who can encourage and pray with you.

Using Prayer Lists to Stay Focused

Prayer lists are an effective tool for organizing your intercessory efforts. They help you track ongoing needs, remember important requests, and stay intentional in your prayers.

How to create and use a prayer list:

1. **Divide requests into categories.** Group needs into areas like family, friends, church, global issues, etc.
2. **Update regularly.** Add new requests and document answers to prayer as they occur.
3. **Review frequently.** Spend time reflecting on your list to ensure no need is overlooked.

Celebrating Progress in Long-Term Prayers

Long-term intercession often involves gradual progress rather than immediate results. Celebrating small victories along the way can encourage you to keep praying and remind you of God's ongoing work.

Ways to celebrate progress:

1. **Thank God for every step forward.** Express gratitude for even the smallest signs of progress.
2. **Record milestones in a prayer journal.** Documenting progress helps you see how God is answering over time.
3. **Share testimonies.** Sharing answered prayers with others builds faith and encourages persistence.

Persistence in prayer is a vital principle of intercession. It requires faith, discipline, and trust in God's perfect timing and purposes. By breaking through spiritual resistance, developing a resilient mindset, and employing practical strategies for consistency, you can persevere in prayer and witness the unfolding of God's promises. Let this principle inspire you to keep knocking, seeking, and trusting, knowing that God is always faithful to respond.

6

Chapter 6

Chapter 6: The Fifth Principle—Standing in the Gap for Others

S tanding in the gap for others is at the heart of intercessory prayer. It is a selfless act of love and faith where we advocate for individuals, families, and communities, asking God to intervene, protect, and restore. This principle emphasizes the power of advocacy, the responsibility to pray for those close to us, and the broader call to intercede for nations and global issues.

Section 1: The Power of Advocacy

Why God Calls Us to Pray for Others

God invites us to intercede for others because it reflects His heart for humanity. In Ezekiel 22:30, God says, *"I looked for someone among them who would build up the wall and stand before me in the gap on behalf of the land so I would not have to destroy it, but I found no one."* This verse illustrates God's desire for intercessors who will advocate on behalf of others, aligning their prayers with His redemptive purposes.

Interceding for others serves several key purposes:

1. **It aligns us with God's compassion.** Intercession allows us to partner with God in extending His love and mercy.
2. **It activates divine intervention.** Our prayers invite God to work in ways that might not occur otherwise (James 5:16).
3. **It fulfills our role as Christ's followers.** Just as Jesus intercedes for us (Romans 8:34), we are called to intercede for others.

The Role of Empathy in Effective Intercession

Empathy is a vital component of standing in the gap. Effective intercession requires us to feel the burdens of those we pray for, approaching God with a heart full of compassion. Jesus modeled this empathy when He wept for Jerusalem (Luke 19:41) and when He prayed for those who crucified Him, saying, *"Father, forgive them, for they do not know what they are doing"* (Luke 23:34).

How to cultivate empathy in intercession:

1. **Spend time understanding the needs of others.** Listen, ask questions, and seek to grasp their struggles.
2. **Allow God to soften your heart.** Ask Him to fill you with His love for the people you are praying for.
3. **Pray with specificity.** Detailed, heartfelt prayers show that you are deeply invested in the person's well-being.

Standing in the Gap as Spiritual Protection

Intercession serves as a form of spiritual protection, shielding others from harm and drawing them closer to God's presence. Job exemplifies this role when he continually offered sacrifices on behalf of his children, saying, *"Perhaps my children have sinned and cursed God in their hearts"* (Job 1:5). His proactive prayers served as a spiritual covering for his family.

Ways to provide spiritual protection through prayer:

1. **Pray for God's guidance and protection.** Ask God to surround those you are interceding for with His presence.

2. **Invoke the armor of God.** Pray Ephesians 6:10-18 over their lives, asking God to equip them for spiritual battles.
3. **Stand firm in faith.** Persist in prayer, trusting that God's power will guard and sustain them.

Section 2: Interceding for Family and Friends

Praying for Specific Needs and Healing

Family and friends are often the first people we think of when interceding, as their needs are close to our hearts. Praying for specific needs, whether they involve physical healing, emotional well-being, or financial provision, allows us to bring their concerns directly to God.

How to pray for specific needs:

1. **Ask for clarity.** Seek to understand the exact nature of their needs so you can pray effectively.
2. **Use Scripture.** Anchor your prayers in promises like Isaiah 41:10: *"Do not fear, for I am with you; do not be dismayed, for I am your God."*
3. **Pray with faith and expectation.** Trust that God hears your prayers and will respond according to His will.

Overcoming Relational Struggles Through Prayer

Relationships often face challenges, including misunderstandings, conflicts, and brokenness. Intercessory prayer can be a powerful tool for healing these struggles. When we pray for restoration, we invite God to work in ways that go beyond human efforts.

Steps to pray for relational healing:

1. **Pray for softened hearts.** Ask God to replace anger, pride, or bitterness with humility and forgiveness.
2. **Invite God's peace.** Use Scriptures like Philippians 4:7 to ask for His peace to guard hearts and minds.
3. **Be persistent.** Relationships often take time to heal, so continue praying

even if progress seems slow.

How to Pray for Salvation and Faith Renewal

One of the most important ways to stand in the gap for family and friends is by praying for their salvation and spiritual growth. God's heart is for everyone to come to a knowledge of Him (1 Timothy 2:4), and our prayers can play a crucial role in that process.

Practical steps for interceding for salvation:

1. **Pray for conviction and openness.** Ask the Holy Spirit to soften their hearts and open their minds to the gospel.
2. **Declare God's promises.** Use Scriptures like Acts 16:31: *"Believe in the Lord Jesus, and you will be saved—you and your household."*
3. **Ask for divine encounters.** Pray that they would experience God's love through people, circumstances, or direct revelation.

Section 3: Interceding for Nations and Communities

Praying for Leaders and Global Issues

God calls us to pray for those in authority and for the welfare of the nations. In 1 Timothy 2:1-2, Paul urges believers to pray *"for kings and all those in authority, that we may live peaceful and quiet lives in all godliness and holiness."* Interceding for leaders and global issues helps advance God's purposes on a broader scale.

How to pray for leaders:

1. **Pray for wisdom and discernment.** Ask God to guide their decisions and give them clarity in leadership.
2. **Seek justice and righteousness.** Pray that leaders would act with integrity and align with God's standards.
3. **Cover them in protection.** Ask God to shield them from harm and surround them with wise counsel.

Using Scripture to Intercede for Justice and Peace

Prayers for justice and peace align with God's heart and His promises. Isaiah 61:8 declares, *"For I, the Lord, love justice; I hate robbery and wrongdoing."* Interceding for justice involves praying for oppressed individuals, communities, and systems to experience God's deliverance.

Examples of scriptural prayers:

1. **For peace:** *"The Lord gives strength to his people; the Lord blesses his people with peace"* (Psalm 29:11).
2. **For justice:** *"Let justice roll on like a river, righteousness like a never-failing stream"* (Amos 5:24).
3. **For mercy:** *"Blessed are the merciful, for they will be shown mercy"* (Matthew 5:7).

Breaking Strongholds Over Cities and Nations

Cities and nations often face spiritual strongholds—patterns of sin, corruption, or oppression that hinder God's purposes. Intercessory prayer can break these strongholds, paving the way for revival and restoration.

How to intercede for cities and nations:

1. **Identify specific needs.** Research the challenges your community or nation faces, such as poverty, violence, or division.
2. **Pray against spiritual strongholds.** Use 2 Corinthians 10:4-5 to declare God's authority over every stronghold.
3. **Call for revival.** Ask God to pour out His Spirit and bring renewal to hearts, families, and institutions.

Standing in the gap for others is a profound privilege and responsibility. Whether you are interceding for family, friends, or nations, your prayers have the power to bring God's presence, peace, and transformation. As you embrace this principle, remember that your advocacy reflects the heart of Jesus, who continually intercedes for us. Let this inspire you to pray boldly and persistently, trusting that God will move through your faithfulness.

7

Chapter 7

Chapter 7: The Sixth Principle—Using Scripture in Intercession

The Word of God is a powerful tool in intercessory prayer. It provides guidance and encouragement and serves as the foundation for effective intercession. Praying Scripture aligns our prayers with God's will, increases our confidence, and releases His power into the situations we are interceding for. This chapter explores the significance of using Scripture in intercession, how to incorporate it into your prayers, and how it unlocks supernatural results.

Section 1: The Power of God's Word

Why Scripture Is Essential for Effective Prayer

Scripture is essential for effective prayer because it reveals God's will and character. Hebrews 4:12 describes the Word of God as *"alive and active, sharper than any double-edged sword."* When we pray Scripture, we echo God's promises, commands, and truths into the situations we are interceding for, ensuring that our prayers align with His purposes.

Key reasons Scripture is indispensable in intercession:

1. **It reflects God's will.** Praying Scripture ensures that our requests are consistent with His divine plan.
2. **It builds faith.** Hearing and declaring God's Word strengthens our confidence in His promises (Romans 10:17).
3. **It is powerful in spiritual warfare.** In Ephesians 6:17, the Word is described as the "sword of the Spirit," equipping us to confront spiritual opposition.

The Transformative Impact of Praying the Word

Praying Scripture is transformative because it aligns our hearts and minds with God's truth. When we pray for God's promises, we declare His authority over our lives and circumstances. For example, when faced with fear, praying Isaiah 41:10—*"Do not fear, for I am with you; do not be dismayed, for I am your God"—*reminds us of God's presence and power, dispelling fear and replacing it with peace.

The transformative power of Scripture includes:

1. **Renewing our minds.** Praying the Word shapes our thoughts and attitudes, aligning them with God's perspective.
2. **Shifting spiritual atmospheres.** Scripture carries the weight of God's authority, driving out darkness and inviting His presence.
3. **Encouraging persistence.** Repeating God's promises during seasons of waiting reinforces our trust in His faithfulness.

Examples of Scriptural Intercession

The Bible is filled with examples of intercessors using Scripture in their prayers. One notable instance is Daniel, who prayed for Israel's restoration by referencing God's covenant promises (Daniel 9:1-19). Similarly, Jesus prayed for His disciples and future believers in John 17, aligning His requests with God's purposes.

These examples teach us:

1. **Scripture is a foundation.** Biblical intercessors often cited God's Word

to remind Him of His promises.

2. **Prayer and Scripture work together.** Combining prayer with Scripture adds depth and power to our intercession.

3. **God responds to His Word.** Praying His Word demonstrates faith in His promises, inviting His intervention.

Section 2: How to Incorporate Scripture

Finding Relevant Verses for Specific Situations

To pray Scripture effectively, it is important to find verses that speak directly to the situation or need you are interceding for. Whether you are praying for healing, provision, or peace, Scripture offers countless promises and principles to guide your prayers.

How to find relevant verses:

1. **Use a concordance or search tool.** Look up keywords related to the situation (e.g., "healing," "peace," "protection").
2. **Seek themes in the Psalms.** The Psalms cover a wide range of emotions and situations, making them a rich resource for intercession.
3. **Ask the Holy Spirit for guidance.** Invite the Spirit to direct you to the passages that align with His purposes.

Example: When praying for someone struggling with anxiety, use Philippians 4:6-7: *"Do not be anxious about anything, but in every situation, by prayer and petition, with thanksgiving, present your requests to God. And the peace of God...will guard your hearts and your minds in Christ Jesus."*

Memorizing Key Scriptures for Intercession

Memorizing Scripture equips you to pray confidently and effectively, even when you do not have a Bible at hand. It also allows God's Word to dwell richly in your heart, shaping your faith and response to challenges.

Tips for memorizing Scripture:

1. **Start small.** Choose one or two verses to focus on each week.
2. **Write them down.** Repetition through writing reinforces memory.
3. **Use them in prayer.** Incorporate memorized verses into your intercession to internalize them further.

Suggested verses to memorize for intercession:

- For strength: *"I can do all this through him who gives me strength"* (Philippians 4:13).
- For healing: *"By his wounds, we are healed"* (Isaiah 53:5).
- For provision: *"And my God will meet all your needs according to the riches of his glory in Christ Jesus"* (Philippians 4:19).

Using Psalms and Promises in Prayer

The Psalms are a treasure trove of prayers that address nearly every human experience, from joy and gratitude to fear and despair. They offer ready-made language for intercession and teach us how to approach God with honesty and reverence.

How to use Psalms in prayer:

1. **Adapt them to specific situations.** Personalize verses to reflect the needs of those you are interceding for.
2. **Pray them verbatim.** Let the words of the Psalmist become your own as you pray for yourself or others.
3. **Combine them with declarations.** Use promises in the Psalms as declarations of faith (e.g., Psalm 23:1: *"The Lord is my shepherd; I lack nothing."*).

Section 3: Unlocking Supernatural Results

How the Word of God Activates Heaven's Power

When we pray Scripture, we activate heaven's power because God's Word carries divine authority. Isaiah 55:11 declares, *"So is my word that goes out from my mouth: It will not return to me empty, but will accomplish what I desire and achieve the purpose for which I sent it."* Praying Scripture ensures that our words align with God's will and invites Him to act on His promises.

How Scripture activates supernatural power:

1. **It commands attention in the spiritual realm.** Demons flee at the declaration of God's Word, and angels respond to it (Psalm 103:20).
2. **It establishes God's will on earth.** By praying Scripture, we partner with God to bring His purposes to fruition.
3. **It strengthens our authority.** Speaking God's Word reminds us of the authority we have in Christ.

Strengthening Faith Through Scriptural Affirmation

Praying Scripture strengthens our faith by continually affirming God's truth over our lives and circumstances. Repeating promises like *"The Lord is my light and my salvation—whom shall I fear?"* (Psalm 27:1) builds confidence and trust, even in challenging situations.

How to use affirmations to strengthen faith:

1. **Speak verses aloud.** Verbalizing Scripture reinforces belief and combats doubt.
2. **Declare them daily.** Make Scripture declarations a regular part of your prayer routine.
3. **Focus on specific promises.** Choose verses that address areas where your faith needs growth.

Turning Scripture Into Declarations

Turning Scripture into declarations transforms prayers into bold statements of faith. Declarations affirm God's sovereignty and invite His power into specific situations.

How to create declarations from Scripture:

1. **Identify the promise.** Choose a verse that applies to the situation.

2. **Personalize it.** Replace general terms with specific names or circumstances.
3. **Speak it with conviction.** Declare the promise with confidence, believing in its truth.

Example:

Original verse: *"The Lord will fight for you; you need only to be still"* (Exodus 14:14).

Declaration: "Lord, I declare that You are fighting for [name]. I trust that Your power is at work, and I rest in Your victory."

Using Scripture in intercession is a transformative practice that aligns our prayers with God's will, strengthens our faith, and releases His power. By grounding your intercession in the Word, you become a conduit for heaven's purposes on earth. Let this principle guide you as you pray, trusting that God's Word will accomplish all He intends.

8

Chapter 8

Chapter 8: The Seventh Principle—Spiritual Warfare in Intercession

Intercessory prayer often involves spiritual warfare as we contend against unseen forces that seek to hinder God's purposes. Ephesians 6:12 reminds us, *"For our struggle is not against flesh and blood, but against the rulers, against the authorities, against the powers of this dark world and against the spiritual forces of evil in the heavenly realms."* Understanding the dynamics of spiritual warfare equips intercessors to pray with authority, perseverance, and victory.

Section 1: Understanding Spiritual Warfare

Identifying Spiritual Battles Through Discernment

Not all challenges are purely physical or circumstantial; many have spiritual roots. Discernment, a gift of the Holy Spirit, is essential for identifying spiritual battles. It enables intercessors to perceive the true nature of the issues they pray about.

How to identify spiritual battles:

1. **Pay attention to patterns.** Recurring issues such as unexplainable conflict, fear, or oppression may indicate spiritual interference.
2. **Seek guidance from the Holy Spirit.** Pray for clarity and ask God to reveal any spiritual dynamics at play.
3. **Use Scripture for confirmation.** The Bible helps us discern whether what we face aligns with the spiritual warfare described in God's Word.

For example, in Acts 16:16-18, Paul discerned an evil spirit fueled a slave girl's fortune-telling. His recognition of the spiritual battle allowed him to confront the issue directly, casting out the spirit in Jesus' name.

Recognizing the Enemy's Tactics in Prayer

The enemy uses deception, distraction, and discouragement to hinder intercessors. John 10:10 reveals his agenda: *"The thief comes only to steal and kill and destroy."* Recognizing these tactics helps intercessors counter them effectively.

Common tactics of the enemy:

1. **Deception.** The enemy plants lies to create fear or doubt. Counter this with the truth of God's Word (John 8:32).
2. **Distraction.** He diverts focus through busyness, mental fog, or irrelevant concerns. Combat this by prioritizing prayer time.
3. **Discouragement.** The enemy magnifies unanswered prayers or setbacks to weaken faith. Respond with perseverance and trust in God's timing.

Why Intercessors Are Front-line Warriors

Intercessors are often at the forefront of spiritual battles because their prayers disrupt the enemy's plans and advance God's kingdom. This role requires courage, endurance, and a willingness to stand firm.

Characteristics of front-line warriors:

1. **Faithful commitment.** Intercessors persist in prayer, knowing their efforts have eternal significance.

2. **Spiritual resilience.** They withstand opposition by relying on God's strength.
3. **Partnership with God.** Intercessors work with God to bring His will to fruition, making them vital in spiritual warfare.

Biblical examples include Moses interceding for Israel during their rebellion (Exodus 32:11-14) and Esther fasting and praying to protect her people (Esther 4:16).

Section 2: Weapons of Spiritual Warfare

The Armor of God as a Prayer Framework

Ephesians 6:13-18 outlines the armor of God, a metaphor for the spiritual tools believers need to stand firm against the enemy. Each piece of armor represents a specific aspect of spiritual readiness, making it an excellent framework for prayer.

How to use the armor of God in intercession:

1. **The belt of truth.** Pray for discernment and the ability to stand on God's truth (John 17:17).
2. **The breastplate of righteousness.** Ask for God's protection over your heart and purity in your motives.
3. **The shoes of peace.** Pray for peace to reign in your mind and relationships as you intercede.
4. **The shield of faith.** Declare your trust in God to extinguish the enemy's fiery darts of doubt and fear.
5. **The helmet of salvation.** Pray for clarity and assurance in your identity as a child of God.
6. **The sword of the Spirit.** Use Scripture to counter the enemy's lies and declare victory.
7. **Prayer in the Spirit.** Allow the Holy Spirit to guide and empower your intercession.

The Power of Fasting and Prayer Together

Fasting enhances prayer by increasing spiritual focus and dependence on God. Throughout Scripture, fasting is linked to breakthroughs in spiritual warfare. For example, in Matthew 17:21, Jesus explained that certain spiritual battles require prayer and fasting.

Why fasting is powerful:

1. **It humbles the spirit.** Fasting reminds us of our dependence on God, clearing the way for His power to work.
2. **It amplifies focus.** Setting aside physical needs creates space for deeper communion with God.
3. **It prepares for spiritual breakthroughs.** Fasting strengthens perseverance and faith, making it a potent weapon in spiritual warfare.

Practical tips for fasting:

- Choose a type of fast (e.g., partial, full, or Daniel fast).
- Begin with a clear purpose, such as seeking God's guidance or breaking a stronghold.
- Combine fasting with increased time in prayer and Scripture reading.

Using Praise and Worship as a Battle Strategy

Praise and worship are powerful tools for overcoming spiritual opposition. They shift our focus from problems to God's greatness, inviting His presence and silencing the enemy. Psalm 22:3 declares that God inhabits the praises of His people, making worship a potent strategy in spiritual warfare.

How to incorporate praise in spiritual warfare:

1. **Declare God's attributes.** Praise Him for His sovereignty, faithfulness, and power.
2. **Sing songs of victory.** Worship reminds us of God's triumph over sin and darkness.
3. **Use Scripture-based praise.** Incorporate verses like Psalm 150:6: *"Let*

everything that has breath praise the Lord."

An example of worship as warfare is in 2 Chronicles 20:21-22, where Jehoshaphat's army sang praises to God, leading to their victory without a fight.

Section 3: Walking in Victory

Declaring Victory Over the Enemy

Victory in spiritual warfare comes through faith and declaration. As intercessors, we do not fight for victory but from victory, knowing that Jesus has already defeated the enemy (Colossians 2:15).

How to declare victory:

1. **Proclaim Jesus' triumph.** Remind the enemy of Christ's victory on the cross.
2. **Speak Scripture over situations.** Declare verses like Romans 8:37: *"In all these things we are more than conquerors through him who loved us."*
3. **Pray with boldness.** Approach God's throne confidently, trusting His promises (Hebrews 4:16).

Testimonies of Triumph Through Intercession

Hearing testimonies of answered prayers and victories in spiritual warfare strengthens faith and encourages persistence. Testimonies remind us that God is faithful and that our prayers are powerful.

Examples of triumph through intercession:

1. **Deliverance from addiction.** Many have experienced freedom from strongholds through the persistent prayers of loved ones.
2. **Restoration of relationships.** Intercession has brought healing to broken families and marriages.
3. **Community transformation.** Prayers for cities and nations have sparked revivals and societal change.

Sharing testimonies:

- Encourage others by recounting answered prayers.
- Document victories in a journal for future reflection.
- Use testimonies to inspire continued intercession.

Remaining Vigilant and Prepared

Spiritual warfare is ongoing, requiring intercessors to remain vigilant and prepared. 1 Peter 5:8 warns, *"Be alert and of sober mind. Your enemy, the devil, prowls around like a roaring lion looking for someone to devour."*

Steps to stay vigilant:

1. **Maintain a strong prayer life.** Regular communication with God strengthens your spiritual defenses.
2. **Stay rooted in Scripture.** Continual study of God's Word equips you for spiritual battles.
3. **Be accountable.** Surround yourself with fellow believers who can support and pray with you.

Spiritual warfare is an integral part of intercessory prayer. When we understand the nature of spiritual battles, wielding the weapons God has provided, and walking in the victory Christ has secured, intercessors can overcome the enemy and advance God's kingdom. Let this principle empower you to pray boldly, persistently, and triumphantly, knowing God is with you in every battle.

9

Chapter 9

Chapter 9: The Role of the Holy Spirit in Intercession

Intercessory prayer is most powerful when it is guided and empowered by the Holy Spirit. The Spirit is not only our Helper and Advocate but also the One who intercedes on our behalf, ensuring that our prayers align with God's will. By partnering with the Spirit, praying in the Spirit, and remaining sensitive to His prompting, we can experience supernatural breakthroughs that transform lives and circumstances.

Section 1: Partnering With the Holy Spirit

The Spirit as Our Helper and Advocate

The Holy Spirit is a vital partner in intercession. Jesus described Him as the Helper, sent to empower and guide believers (John 14:16-17). The Spirit strengthens us when we feel weak, provides wisdom when we lack understanding and advocates for us before the Father.

Key roles of the Spirit in intercession:

1. **He equips us to pray effectively.** The Spirit illuminates Scripture, giving us insight into God's promises and purposes.

47

2. **He strengthens our faith.** When we are weary or uncertain, the Spirit provides the boldness to persevere.
3. **He intercedes for us.** Romans 8:26-27 states, *"The Spirit helps us in our weakness. We do not know what we ought to pray for, but the Spirit himself intercedes for us through wordless groans."*

Partnering with the Spirit requires acknowledging His presence and seeking His guidance in every aspect of intercession.

How the Spirit Intercedes on Our Behalf

The Spirit's intercession is both profound and mysterious. He prays on our behalf when we are unable to articulate our needs or when we lack understanding of the situation. His prayers are perfect, aligned with the will of God, and free of human limitations.

Benefits of the Spirit's intercession:

1. **He bridges the gap.** The Spirit communicates our deepest needs to the Father, even when we cannot express them.
2. **He ensures alignment with God's will.** His prayers are always consistent with God's purposes.
3. **He brings comfort and peace.** Knowing that the Spirit intercedes for us provides assurance and confidence in prayer.

Relying on the Spirit for Guidance in Prayer

Effective intercession depends on our reliance on the Spirit for guidance. He reveals what to pray for, how to pray, and when to pray, enabling us to align with God's timing and purposes.

How to rely on the Spirit:

1. **Begin with surrender.** Invite the Holy Spirit to lead your prayer time, laying aside your agenda.
2. **Listen actively.** Be still and attentive, allowing the Spirit to impress specific needs or Scriptures on your heart.

3. **Trust His direction.** Even when His guidance seems unexpected, follow with faith, knowing that He sees the full picture.

Section 2: Praying in the Spirit

The Role of Tongues in Intercessory Prayer

Praying in tongues is a unique and powerful way to engage in intercessory prayer. This gift, described in 1 Corinthians 14:2, allows believers to communicate directly with God in a heavenly language that transcends human understanding.

Benefits of praying in tongues:

1. **It bypasses human limitations.** Tongues enable believers to pray beyond their knowledge or vocabulary.
2. **It builds spiritual strength.** Paul wrote in 1 Corinthians 14:4 that praying in tongues edifies the spirit.
3. **It aligns with God's will.** The Spirit prays through us in perfect harmony with God's purposes (Romans 8:27).

How to incorporate tongues into intercession:

1. **Ask for the gift.** If you have not yet received this gift, pray for it, trusting that the Spirit gives freely (Luke 11:13).
2. **Use tongues when words fail.** Allow the Spirit to take over when you are unsure how to pray.
3. **Combine tongues with understanding.** Alternate between praying in tongues and praying in your native language for a balanced approach.

Recognizing Spirit-Led Impressions and Burdens

The Holy Spirit often leads intercessors by placing impressions or burdens on their hearts. These may come as a sudden thought, a deep sense of compassion, or an unshakable conviction to pray for a specific person or situation.

How to recognize Spirit-led impressions:

1. **Pay attention to recurring thoughts.** If a name or issue keeps coming to mind, it may be the Spirit prompting you to pray.
2. **Be sensitive to emotional burdens.** A sudden heaviness or urgency in your spirit can indicate a call to intercede.
3. **Test impressions with Scripture.** Ensure that what you sense aligns with God's Word.

Responding to Spirit-led burdens:

1. **Pray immediately.** Act on the prompting as soon as possible, trusting the Spirit's timing.
2. **Seek clarity through prayer.** Ask the Spirit for specific directions on how to intercede.
3. **Trust the outcome to God.** Release the burden to Him, knowing that He is in control.

Staying Attuned to the Spirit's Leading

Staying attuned to the Holy Spirit requires cultivating a deep relationship with Him through prayer, worship, and the study of Scripture. It involves living in a state of spiritual awareness, ready to respond to His guidance at any moment.

Practical steps to stay attuned:

1. **Maintain a posture of surrender.** Begin each day by inviting the Spirit to lead you.
2. **Create space for stillness.** Regular times of silence allow you to hear the Spirit's whisper.
3. **Remain open to surprises.** The Spirit may lead in unexpected ways; be willing to follow wherever He directs.

Section 3: Experiencing Supernatural Breakthroughs

Stories of Spirit-Driven Intercessions

Testimonies of Spirit-driven intercession reveal the power of partnering with the Holy Spirit. These stories demonstrate how His guidance leads to miraculous outcomes that glorify God and transform lives.

Examples of Spirit-driven intercession:

1. **A timely prayer for protection.** Many believers recount sensing an urgent need to pray for someone, only to discover later that their prayers coincided with a critical moment of danger.
2. **Healing through Spirit-led prayer.** Testimonies of physical and emotional healing often result from intercessors praying as the Spirit directs.
3. **Salvation and restoration.** The Spirit's prompting to pray for a wayward loved one has brought many back to faith and reconciliation with God.

Miracles That Happen When the Spirit Moves

When the Holy Spirit moves through intercession, miracles happen. Whether it is a supernatural provision, a breakthrough in a seemingly impossible situation, or a life changed by God's power, the results of Spirit-led prayer are undeniable.

Examples of Spirit-driven miracles:

1. **Breaking generational strongholds.** Spirit-led prayers have freed families from cycles of addiction, abuse, or poverty.
2. **Transforming communities.** Intercessors praying for revival have seen entire neighborhoods or regions changed by the power of God.
3. **Opening doors for the gospel.** Spirit-led intercession often prepares the way for evangelism and discipleship.

Remaining Sensitive to the Spirit's Prompting

Sensitivity to the Holy Spirit is key to sustaining supernatural breakthroughs. This involves remaining connected to Him through ongoing prayer, worship, and obedience.

How to stay sensitive to the Spirit:

1. **Cultivate humility.** Recognize your dependence on the Spirit for guidance and power.
2. **Live in gratitude.** Thank the Spirit for His presence and work in your life.
3. **Seek continual renewal.** Ask for a fresh filling of the Spirit daily to remain empowered and attuned.

The Holy Spirit is the ultimate guide and power source for intercessory prayer. By partnering with Him, praying in the Spirit, and remaining sensitive to His leading, intercessors can experience supernatural breakthroughs that reveal God's glory and advance His kingdom. Let this principle inspire you to deepen your relationship with the Spirit, trusting Him to lead you into greater effectiveness and joy in intercession.

10

Chapter 10

Chapter 10: The Role of Fasting in Intercession

Fasting is a powerful spiritual discipline that enhances intercessory prayer by increasing focus, humility, and dependence on God. It is more than abstaining from food—it is an intentional act of drawing closer to God and aligning with His purposes. When combined with prayer, fasting unlocks breakthroughs, strengthens faith, and deepens intimacy with God. This chapter explores why fasting amplifies prayer, practical steps to engage in fasting, and testimonies of how fasting has transformed lives and circumstances.

Section 1: Why Fasting Amplifies Prayer

Biblical Examples of Fasting and Breakthroughs

The Bible is filled with examples of fasting that led to significant spiritual breakthroughs, demonstrating its effectiveness in intercessory prayer.

1. **Moses on Mount Sinai.** Moses fasted for 40 days while receiving the Ten Commandments (Exodus 34:28). His fasting signified reverence and dependence on God during a critical moment in Israel's history.

2. **Esther's fast for deliverance.** Queen Esther called for a three-day fast before approaching the king to save the Jewish people (Esther 4:16). The fast united the community in seeking God's intervention and resulted in a miraculous deliverance.

3. **Jesus' fast in the wilderness.** Jesus fasted for 40 days and nights before beginning His public ministry (Matthew 4:1-11). This period of fasting prepared Him spiritually for the challenges ahead and reinforced His authority over temptation.

These examples highlight how fasting prepares believers for significant moments, amplifies their prayers, and invites God's power into challenging situations.

How Fasting Increases Spiritual Focus

Fasting sharpens the spiritual focus by removing distractions and creating space to hear God more clearly. In a world filled with noise and busyness, fasting quiets the soul, allowing believers to concentrate fully on God.

Key ways fasting increases focus:

1. **Simplifies life.** By stepping away from the physical need for food or other comforts, fasting clears mental and emotional space for prayer and reflection.

2. **Humbles the spirit.** Fasting acknowledges our dependence on God, shifting our attention from worldly concerns to divine priorities.

3. **Enhances spiritual sensitivity.** Many believers report heightened awareness of God's presence and guidance during fasting.

Joel 2:12 encapsulates this focus: *"Even now," declares the Lord, "return to me with all your heart, with fasting and weeping and mourning."*

Strengthening Faith Through Fasting

Fasting builds faith by fostering reliance on God for strength, sustenance, and breakthroughs. As physical hunger reminds us of our spiritual dependence, fasting becomes a practical exercise in trusting God's provision.

How fasting strengthens faith:

1. **Reinforces God's power.** Fasting shifts reliance from physical resources to God's supernatural ability.
2. **Overcomes doubt.** Persisting in fasting during challenging times strengthens belief in God's promises.
3. **Builds perseverance.** Fasting teaches endurance, mirroring the persistence needed for long-term intercession.

Isaiah 58:6 highlights the transformative power of fasting: *"Is not this the kind of fasting I have chosen: to loose the chains of injustice and untie the cords of the yoke, to set the oppressed free and break every yoke?"*

Section 2: Practical Fasting Guidelines

Different Types of Fasts and Their Purposes

Fasting can take various forms, each suited to different purposes and physical conditions. Understanding the types of fasts helps believers choose one that aligns with their spiritual goals.

Types of fasts:

1. **Complete fast.** Abstaining from all food and drinking only water. This type requires careful preparation and should be done for shorter periods unless medically supervised.
2. **Partial fast.** Restricting certain types of food, such as in the Daniel Fast, which involves eating only fruits, vegetables, and water (Daniel 1:12).
3. **Intermittent fast.** Fasting during specific times of the day, such as skipping one or two meals while maintaining a prayerful focus.
4. **Non-food fast.** Abstaining from non-essential activities, such as social media, entertainment, or other distractions, to dedicate time to prayer and reflection.

Each type of fast serves as a means to deepen reliance on God and prioritize spiritual over physical needs.

Preparing Your Body and Spirit for Fasting

Preparation is essential for a successful fast, ensuring that both your body and spirit are ready for the experience.

Steps to prepare for fasting:

1. **Set a clear purpose.** Define why you are fasting, such as seeking clarity, interceding for someone, or deepening your relationship with God.
2. **Start gradually.** If fasting is new to you, begin with shorter fasts and increase the duration over time.
3. **Pray for strength.** Ask God to sustain you physically and spiritually during the fast.
4. **Adjust your diet.** In the days leading up to a fast, eat lighter meals and drink plenty of water to prepare your body.

Spiritual preparation includes spending time in prayer, reading Scripture, and asking the Holy Spirit to guide you throughout the fast.

Overcoming Challenges During a Fast

Fasting often comes with physical, emotional, and spiritual challenges, but perseverance through these difficulties leads to growth and breakthroughs.

Common challenges and solutions:

1. **Physical hunger.** Drink water and remind yourself of the spiritual purpose behind the fast.
2. **Mental distractions.** Refocus through Scripture and prayer whenever your mind wanders.
3. **Spiritual opposition.** Expect resistance from the enemy and counter it with Scripture, such as Ephesians 6:10-18.
4. **Fatigue or discouragement.** Rest when needed and lean on God for renewed strength.

Matthew 6:16-18 encourages believers to fast with humility and a focus on God, assuring us that *"your Father, who sees what is done in secret, will reward you."*

Section 3: Testimonies of Fasting and Intercession

Real-Life Stories of Breakthrough Through Fasting

Testimonies of fasting reveal its transformative power in intercession, inspiring faith and perseverance in others.

1. **Healing through fasting.** One family fasted and prayed for a loved one diagnosed with a terminal illness. After weeks of focused prayer and fasting, the individual experienced complete healing, leaving doctors amazed and the family strengthened in their faith.
2. **Spiritual revival.** A church community engaged in a 21-day fast, seeking God's guidance and revival. During the fast, they witnessed a renewed sense of unity, salvation, and growth in spiritual gifts.
3. **Deliverance from addiction.** A man struggling with addiction committed to fasting and prayer, asking God for freedom. Through his fast, he gained the strength to overcome his struggle, testifying to the power of God's intervention.

How Fasting Deepens Intimacy With God

Fasting creates a sacred space for believers to connect with God on a deeper level. By setting aside physical needs, fasting allows for heightened spiritual awareness and intimacy.

Ways fasting deepens intimacy:

1. **Increased dependence on God.** Hunger and weakness remind us of our reliance on His strength and provision.
2. **Clarity in hearing God's voice.** The quietness of fasting fosters an environment where believers can discern God's guidance.
3. **A deeper understanding of His heart.** Fasting aligns us with God's

priorities, allowing us to share in His burden for the world.

Psalm 42:1 captures this longing: *"As the deer pants for streams of water, so my soul pants for you, my God."*

Encouragement to Make Fasting a Lifestyle

Fasting is not just an occasional practice but can become a regular part of a believer's spiritual life. By incorporating fasting into your routine, you create ongoing opportunities for renewal, breakthroughs, and intimacy with God.

Tips for making fasting a lifestyle:

1. **Schedule regular fasts.** Commit to fasting weekly, monthly, or seasonally as part of your spiritual rhythm.
2. **Fast with community.** Join others in fasting for shared purposes, such as revival or interceding for global needs.
3. **Celebrate the results.** Reflect on how fasting has impacted your spiritual life and the lives of those you intercede for.

Fasting is a powerful discipline that amplifies prayer, strengthens faith, and deepens intimacy with God. By understanding its purpose, preparing effectively, and persevering through challenges, believers can experience extraordinary breakthroughs in intercession. Let the testimonies of fasting inspire you to embrace this practice, trusting that God rewards those who seek Him with their whole heart.

11

Chapter 11

Chapter 11: Measuring the Impact of Intercessory Prayer

The practice of intercessory prayer is deeply rewarding, not only because it aligns us with God's will but also because it produces tangible results in the spiritual and physical realms. Recognizing the impact of intercession helps sustain faith, build community, and inspire others to engage in prayer. This chapter explores how to measure the effectiveness of intercessory prayer through gratitude, testimonies, and encouraging others to become intercessors.

Section 1: Recognizing God's Hand in Answers

Identifying God's Response to Prayers

One of the most fulfilling aspects of intercessory prayer is witnessing how God answers. Sometimes, His responses are immediate and unmistakable, while at other times, they unfold gradually. Recognizing His hand in these answers requires spiritual discernment and an attitude of attentiveness.

Ways to identify God's response to prayers:

1. **Be observant.** Pay attention to changes in the circumstances or people

you have been praying for. Often, subtle shifts signal God's hand at work.

2. **Keep a prayer journal.** Documenting prayer requests and outcomes makes it easier to track answered prayers. Review these entries periodically to see how God has moved.

3. **Pray for discernment.** Ask the Holy Spirit to help you recognize answers that may not align with your expectations but fulfill God's greater purpose.

Sometimes, God's response is "yes," bringing immediate resolution, while at other times, His answer is "no" or "wait." Trusting His wisdom and sovereignty is essential for maintaining faith amid unanswered prayers or delayed outcomes.

The Role of Gratitude in Sustaining Faith

Gratitude plays a crucial role in sustaining faith throughout the process of intercessory prayer. By thanking God for what He has done and will do, we shift our focus from unmet needs to His faithfulness and provision.

How Gratitude Strengthens Faith:

1. **Acknowledges God's sovereignty.** Gratitude reinforces our trust in God's control over every situation.

2. **Keeps our hearts aligned with His will.** When we thank God even for unanswered prayers, we demonstrate submission to His timing and purposes.

3. **Encourages perseverance.** Reflecting on past answered prayers through gratitude motivates us to continue praying with confidence.

Philippians 4:6 emphasizes this principle: *"Do not be anxious about anything, but in every situation, by prayer and petition, with thanksgiving, present your requests to God."*

Celebrating Both Small and Large Victories

No victory in prayer is too small to celebrate. Whether it is a minor breakthrough or a monumental answer, each result reflects God's faithfulness and care. Celebrating these victories builds faith and reminds us of His goodness.

Practical ways to celebrate answered prayers:

1. **Offer thanks in prayer.** Dedicate time to praise and thank God for His intervention.
2. **Share the testimony.** Let others know how God has answered your prayers, inspiring them to trust Him more.
3. **Mark the occasion.** Create tangible reminders of God's faithfulness, such as journaling, creating a prayer board, or holding a celebration with fellow intercessors.

Celebrating victories also helps us remain hopeful during seasons of waiting, as it reminds us that God is always at work, even when we cannot see it.

Section 2: Sharing Testimonies

How Testimonies Encourage Others to Pray

Sharing testimonies of answered prayers is one of the most effective ways to encourage others to engage in intercession. Testimonies reveal the power of prayer and God's faithfulness, inspiring others to seek Him with greater boldness.

Why testimonies are powerful:

1. **They build faith.** Hearing how God has worked in others' lives reminds believers of His ability to do the same for them.
2. **They demonstrate God's goodness.** Testimonies highlight the personal nature of God's care and provision.
3. **They provide evidence of prayer's effectiveness.** Stories of answered prayers show that intercession produces real results.

When sharing a testimony, be specific about the situation, the prayer offered, and the outcome. This level of detail helps listeners connect with the story and strengthens their belief in God's power.

Building Community Through Shared Stories

Testimonies not only inspire individuals but also foster a sense of community among believers. Sharing stories of answered prayers within a prayer group, church, or fellowship creates a culture of encouragement and mutual faith-building.

How shared testimonies build community:

1. **They strengthen relationships.** Hearing each other's experiences deepens bonds and fosters spiritual unity.
2. **They motivate collective prayer.** When a group sees the results of intercession, members are more likely to commit to praying together.
3. **They create a ripple effect.** Encouraged by others' testimonies, more people are inspired to pray and share their own stories.

Consider dedicating time during group meetings to share updates on prayer requests and celebrate God's work collectively. This practice keeps the group focused and energized.

Honoring God by Declaring His Works

Sharing testimonies is also an act of worship that honors God. Psalm 66:16 declares, *"Come and hear, all you who fear God; let me tell you what he has done for me."* When we testify to His faithfulness, we glorify Him and proclaim His greatness to others.

Ways to honor God through testimonies:

1. **Speak with humility.** Acknowledge that the outcome is solely due to God's power and grace.
2. **Focus on His character.** Highlight how the experience revealed His love, faithfulness, or provision.
3. **Invite others to respond.** Encourage listeners to trust God with their

own needs and challenges.

Testimonies are a powerful witness to both believers and non-believers, showcasing God's presence and activity in the world today.

Section 3: Encouraging Others to Intercede

Mentoring and Teaching the Next Generation

One of the most impactful ways to measure the legacy of intercessory prayer is by mentoring others to become intercessors themselves. Teaching the next generation of believers to pray boldly and effectively ensures that the power of intercession continues to shape lives and communities.

How to mentor others in intercession:

1. **Lead by example.** Model a consistent and passionate prayer life.
2. **Teach practical skills.** Share methods for studying Scripture, discerning God's will, and praying with persistence.
3. **Encourage participation.** Invite others to join you in prayer, gradually increasing their confidence and involvement.

Mentoring younger believers in prayer also equips them to face spiritual challenges with faith and resilience, leaving a lasting impact on their lives.

Creating Prayer Groups and Movements

Another way to encourage intercession is by forming prayer groups or movements that unite believers around shared goals. These groups provide accountability, support, and a collective sense of purpose in prayer.

Steps to create a prayer group:

1. **Define the mission.** Identify the focus of the group, such as praying for families, churches, or global issues.
2. **Invite participants.** Reach out to like-minded believers who share a passion for intercession.

3. **Establish a rhythm.** Schedule regular meetings to pray together and share updates on prayer requests.

Prayer movements have the potential to spark revival, bring transformation to communities, and address pressing global concerns. By creating opportunities for collective intercession, you expand the reach and impact of prayer.

Leaving a Legacy of Faithful Intercession

A life devoted to intercessory prayer leaves a lasting legacy that impacts generations. Whether through the prayers you have prayed, the testimonies you have shared, or the people you have mentored, your commitment to intercession becomes a powerful witness to God's faithfulness.

How to leave a legacy of prayer:

1. **Document your journey.** Keep a record of prayer requests, answers, and testimonies to inspire others long after you are gone.
2. **Empower others.** Equip and encourage future intercessors to carry on the ministry of prayer.
3. **Pray for future generations.** Dedicate time to intercede for the spiritual growth and well-being of your family, church, and community.

Your legacy is not measured by the number of prayers you have prayed but by the lives transformed through your obedience and faithfulness.

Recognizing the impact of intercessory prayer is a vital part of the prayer journey. By identifying God's answers, sharing testimonies, and inspiring others to intercede, you participate in a ripple effect that extends far beyond your own life. Let this chapter encourage you to celebrate the victories, honor God's work, and invest in the next generation of intercessors, ensuring that the power of prayer continues to bring transformation for years to come.

12

Chapter 12

Chapter 12: Sustaining a Life of Intercession

Intercessory prayer is not a short-term commitment; it is a lifelong calling that requires perseverance, growth, and spiritual renewal. Sustaining a life of intercession involves staying spiritually fresh, continuing to grow in your relationship with God, and leaving a lasting impact that inspires others. This chapter offers practical guidance for maintaining a vibrant prayer life and ensuring that your intercession continues to bear fruit for generations to come.

Section 1: Staying Spiritually Fresh

Avoiding Burnout in Long-Term Intercession

Long-term intercession can be demanding, and without intentional care, intercessors may experience burnout. Physical fatigue, emotional exhaustion, and spiritual dryness are common challenges, but they can be overcome with proactive strategies.

How to avoid burnout:

1. **Set realistic boundaries.** Balance your prayer life with other responsibil-

ities, and recognize that you are not solely responsible for the outcomes.

2. **Prioritize self-care.** Adequate rest, healthy eating, and physical activity support both your body and mind.

3. **Seek support.** Share burdens with fellow intercessors, allowing them to pray for you and with you.

Galatians 6:9 encourages perseverance: *"Let us not become weary in doing good, for at the proper time we will reap a harvest if we do not give up."*

Renewing Your Spirit Through Worship and Rest

Worship and rest are essential for spiritual renewal. Worship focuses your heart on God's greatness, shifting your perspective from the demands of intercession to the sufficiency of His power. Rest, both physical and spiritual, allows you to recharge and remain effective in your calling.

Practical ways to renew your spirit:

1. **Engage in worship daily.** Whether through music, Scripture, or silent reflection, worship cultivates joy and gratitude.

2. **Practice Sabbath rest.** Dedicate time each week to step away from responsibilities and focus on God.

3. **Spend time in nature.** Creation often provides a peaceful setting for reflection and renewal.

Matthew 11:28-30 offers comfort: *"Come to me, all you who are weary and burdened, and I will give you rest."*

Remaining Rooted in God's Word

God's Word is a constant source of strength and direction for intercessors. By remaining rooted in Scripture, you build a firm foundation for your prayers and ensure that your intercession aligns with God's will.

How to stay rooted in the Word:

1. **Read daily.** Consistent Bible reading keeps your heart and mind attuned

to God's voice.

2. **Meditate on key passages.** Reflecting on Scriptures related to prayer deepens your understanding and encourages faith.
3. **Memorize verses.** Having Scripture readily available in your heart equips you to pray effectively in any situation.

Psalm 1:2-3 describes the benefits of staying rooted in God's Word: *"Blessed is the one...whose delight is in the law of the Lord, and who meditates on his law day and night. That person is like a tree planted by streams of water."*

Section 2: Continuing to Grow in Prayer

Exploring Deeper Levels of Intimacy With God

Intercession is not just about presenting requests; it is about developing a deeper relationship with God. As you grow in intimacy with Him, your prayers become more aligned with His heart and His purposes.

How to deepen your intimacy with God:

1. **Spend time in silence.** Quieting your heart allows you to hear God's voice more clearly.
2. **Seek His presence.** Focus on simply being with God rather than bringing a list of requests.
3. **Invite the Holy Spirit.** Ask the Spirit to reveal more of God's character and will as you pray.

Psalm 42:1 expresses this longing: *"As the deer pants for streams of water, so my soul pants for you, my God."*

Learning From Other Intercessors' Experiences

There is much to learn from those who have walked the path of intercession before you. Their wisdom, testimonies, and strategies can inspire and equip you for greater effectiveness in prayer.

Ways to learn from other intercessors:

1. **Read biographies.** Explore the lives of great intercessors like George Müller, Hudson Taylor, or Rees Howells.
2. **Join prayer groups.** Participating in a community of intercessors allows you to observe and adopt new practices.
3. **Seek mentorship.** Ask experienced intercessors for guidance and encouragement.

Proverbs 27:17 emphasizes the value of shared wisdom: *"As iron sharpens iron, so one person sharpens another."*

Embracing Lifelong Learning in Prayer

Prayer is a dynamic and ever-evolving discipline. Embracing a posture of lifelong learning keeps your intercession fresh, effective, and aligned with God's will.

How to continue growing in prayer:

1. **Study books on prayer.** Read works by authors like E.M. Bounds, Andrew Murray, or modern writers on intercession.
2. **Attend workshops and conferences.** Learning from prayer leaders and practitioners broadens your perspective.
3. **Experiment with new methods.** Explore creative approaches, such as journaling, prayer walks, or Scripture-based prayer.

Philippians 3:12 reminds us to keep pressing forward: *"Not that I have already obtained all this, or have already arrived at my goal, but I press on to take hold of that for which Christ Jesus took hold of me."*

Section 3: Leaving a Lasting Impact

Inspiring Future Generations Through Prayer

Your commitment to intercession can inspire future generations to embrace a life of prayer. By modeling faithfulness and passion in your own prayer life, you encourage others to follow in your footsteps.

Ways to inspire future generations:

1. **Pray with children.** Teach young people to pray by involving them in simple, age-appropriate intercession.
2. **Share stories of answered prayers.** Testimonies of God's faithfulness build faith in those who hear them.
3. **Encourage curiosity.** Invite questions about prayer and provide resources to help others grow.

Psalm 78:4 underscores the importance of passing on faith: *"We will tell the next generation the praiseworthy deeds of the Lord, his power, and the wonders he has done."*

Building a Legacy of Miracles and Faith

A life devoted to intercessory prayer leaves a legacy of miracles and faith that continues to impact others long after you are gone. Your prayers plant seeds that can bear fruit for generations, bringing transformation and blessing to those you have interceded for.

How to build a legacy:

1. **Document your prayers.** Keep a record of your intercessory efforts, including answered prayers and testimonies.
2. **Invest in others.** Mentor and disciple individuals who can carry on the ministry of intercession.
3. **Focus on eternal impact.** Pray for outcomes that align with God's kingdom purposes.

Hebrews 11:4 reminds us that faith leaves a legacy: *"By faith, Abel still speaks, even though he is dead."*

Trusting God With the Results of Your Prayers

Leaving a lasting impact requires surrendering the results of your prayers to God. While you may not see every outcome in your lifetime, trusting God ensures that your intercession aligns with His greater plan.

How to trust God with the results:

1. **Let go of control.** Recognize that your role is to pray, not to dictate the outcome.
2. **Believe in God's timing.** Trust that He answers perfectly at the perfect time.
3. **Rest in His sovereignty.** Know that God's plans are always for the ultimate good of those who love Him.

Isaiah 55:11 offers reassurance: *"So is my word that goes out from my mouth: It will not return to me empty, but will accomplish what I desire and achieve the purpose for which I sent it."*

Sustaining a life of intercession requires spiritual renewal, continual growth, and a focus on leaving a lasting impact. By staying spiritually fresh, deepening your relationship with God, and inspiring others, you can ensure that your prayers contribute to God's purposes for generations to come. Let this chapter encourage you to embrace intercession as a lifelong calling, trusting that your faithfulness will bear fruit in ways that glorify God and transform lives.

13

Conclusion

Conclusion

Intercessory prayer is a divine privilege and a powerful tool for partnering with God to bring His will to earth. As you have journeyed through the principles of faith-filled prayer, aligning with God's will, praying with boldness and persistence, standing in the gap for others, using Scripture, engaging in spiritual warfare, relying on the Holy Spirit, fasting, and leaving a legacy, you have been equipped to step boldly into your calling as an intercessor.

This journey is not without challenges, but it is one of eternal significance. Your prayers are shaping lives, transforming circumstances, and advancing God's kingdom in ways you may not always see but can trust are making an impact. Continue to approach God's throne with confidence, persist in faith, and rely on His Spirit to guide you.

May your intercession become a source of joy, intimacy with God, and spiritual power. Remember, your prayers matter. When heaven hears, mountains move.

Epilogue

Epilogue

As you close this book, consider how you can integrate these principles into your daily life. Reflect on the ways God has already used your prayers and dream about what He will do through your faithfulness. The call to intercession is not just for a moment or a season—it is a lifestyle that grows deeper and richer as you walk with God.

Let this book be a springboard into a life of powerful, transformative prayer. Whether you are praying for a loved one, your community, or the world, know that God hears every word, and your intercession has the power to change the course of lives and history.

Take the time to dedicate your prayer journey to God. Ask Him to open your eyes to His purposes and give you the strength and courage to stand in the gap for others. May your intercession glorify Him and bring His light to the world.

Afterword

Afterword

As you reach the final page of this book, I want to thank you for embarking on this journey of intercessory prayer. Writing this book has been both a labor of love and an act of obedience to God's call. My hope and prayer is that the insights, principles, and stories shared here will empower you to step boldly into your role as an intercessor.

Prayer is a gift, a bridge between heaven and earth that allows us to partner with God in ways that transcend our understanding. As you continue your prayer journey, remember that every whispered plea, every bold declaration, and every persistent intercession reaches the ears of a loving and attentive God. He is not only able to respond but delights in doing so.

This is not the end of your journey but a new chapter. Keep pressing in, keep seeking, and keep trusting. Your prayers matter, and the impact they create will ripple into eternity.

About the Author

About the Author

Dr. Ferris Corbett, DrPH, is a passionate advocate for the transformative power of prayer. With years of experience as an intercessor and prayer leader, Dr. Corbett, DrPH, has dedicated their life to equipping believers to engage in bold, faith-filled intercession that brings heaven's power to earth.

A lifelong student of God's Word, Dr. Corbett, DrPH draws from Scripture, personal experiences, and testimonies of answered prayers to inspire and teach others. Known for their ability to make complex spiritual truths accessible and practical, Dr. Corbett, DrPH, has taught extensively on prayer and discipleship, serving as a resource for believers seeking to deepen their faith.

In addition to writing, Dr. Corbett, DrPH, speaks at churches, conferences, and retreats, where they encourage others to embrace their calling as intercessors. Their ministry focuses on igniting a passion for prayer, fostering spiritual growth, and creating a legacy of faithful intercession.

When not writing or speaking, Dr. Corbett, DrPH, enjoys flying drones, spending time in quiet reflection, studying the Bible, and nurturing meaningful connections with family and friends. They believe wholeheartedly in the promise of James 5:16: *"The prayer of a righteous person is powerful and effective."*

Dr. Corbett, DrPH, resides in South Carolina and can be reached at universal deliverance2@gmail.com for speaking engagements, resources, or prayer inquiries.